MIRRAN THOUGHT

MIRRAN THOUGHT

Spitzwiesenstr. 50
90765 Fürth
Germany

www.dwmirran.de
www.empty.de
empty@empty.de

READ EIGHTEEN (MT-609)

Printed by BOD
In de Tarpen 42
D-22848 Norderstedt
www.bod.de
info@bod.de
ISBN 978-3-7448-0970-2

First printing 2017

MIRRAN THOUGHT is the publishing arm of Mirran Threat, a company devoted to releasing the music and writings of the various members of Doc Wör Mirran. Mirran Thought and Mirran Threat are both divisions of MT Undertainment.

THE CUNNILINGUIST

Western Haiku, Volume 8

Joseph B. Raimond

These pieces were written in 2010 and
2011 in:
Regensburg, Harz, Hamburg and
Munich, Germany.
Adine, Sterzing and Florence, Italy.
Basel, Switzerland.
Swinemünde, Poland.
Vienna, Austria.

As always, in loving memory of Frank
Abendroth.

Dedicated to Nicholas Winton

Cover art by Joseph B. Raimond, from
the "Tourist" series of acrylic paintings,
Malcesine Italy, 2017.

This is DWM release Nr. 153

Regensburg

You know you're an old man
When the hairs growing out of
Your nose start to turn grey

The falling autumn leaves
Get glued to the sidewalk
By the guts of stepped-on slugs

That little boy, so secure
In the back seat of the car, asleep
Died a long time ago

Old drunk, playing harmonica
Annoyed waiting passengers
But I thought he was pretty good

Give the stupid fly an aspirin
After banging his head so often
On my kitchen window

That ancient stone bridge carried
Knights and Nazis, hippies, punks
Now carries me

Tired to the bone
The old man lay down
With guilt, ringing in his ears

Grey tiles and the smell of soap
Reminds me of a little boy
Bathing in Grandma's tub

The drunken party friends of today
If they don't grow up
Are the city's bums of tomorrow

Pressed back in your seat, a roar
Speed bumpy, speed smooth
Nose to the sky, another take-off

Why can't you see, the folly of
Uncle Sam, its lies and dirt
Killing us, slowly

That little boy, so in love with
The smell of freshly mowed grass
Died a long time ago

„Hey, it's punk rock, dude"
Is just as dumb as
„My faith in the lord"

Excuse me, but I'm very busy
Falling in love with a waitress
I'll never see again

Haiku as a more artistic, perhaps
Arrogant form of
T-shirt and bumper sticker slogans

Munich

The river of blood
Drawn down the steep road
By a cruel force of gravity

The hunchback on fire
Hobbled to call 911
But no one cared nor came

Birthing death
Not even conservative Republicans
Expected her to keep her baby

Our fleeting technology
So important, yet so temporary
Destined to be obsolete, unwanted

I was to write volumes
Of inspired text
That no one will ever read

The Nazi was quizzical
Scratched his bald head
And injured his one brain cell

The terrorist exploded
Spreading his organs in hate
Among the innocent of the world

Don't dare believe the Nazi
Who claims he is harmless
Just a beer drinking buddy

Death as a prostitute
Will fuck you till you die
And you still will have to pay her!

A depressed fatso
Sulking in the moonlit mist
Can still evoke grace

You know you're getting
To be an old artist
When you start to inspire yourself

If I consider your stature
Then I am convinced
Humans evolved from toads

A blissful trudge
He walks the streets in happiness
Oblivious to the angry stares

Self-portrait as a burn victim
Let me show you
What I really look like

The terrorist exploded
Spreading his organs of hate
Among the guilty of the world

The dancing ugly
Is used to dancing alone
The dance floor to himself

A long night drive, cool music
Is fuel for loneliness
A recipe for inspiration

A young boy's memory
An injured cyclist,
A crushed helmet, a river of blood

The spider with cleavage
Don't catch many flies
But horny biologists love her

The ghost of sex
The ghosts of hardons past
Haunts the crippled old man

The modesty of the Americans
Their fear of nakedness, unlimited
Sponsored by Sears & Roebuck

A depressed fairy
Has trouble flying,
Doesn't twinkle in the moonlight

Walking the dark, wet streets of
Munich, I didn't meet any
Of your fabled arrogant Bavarians

That long drive home
Those last few miles
Are the longest and hardest

When death burns
We all suffer
In our graves

His mother was an insect
His dad a spider
He caught and ate himself

Adine

The dried mud of a Siena hillside
Inspiration to generations
Of artists and paint manufacturers

Don't be a fool,
Just relax, lay down and die
And don't question mother nature

I am as an oil shimmer
In a curbside puddle
Spreading my art so thin

I find solace in the big bang
For at least there
We were one, together in spirit

A dusty dirt road
Un-named
Leading to nowhere important

The American redneck
Got an even redder neck
On his Florida beach holiday

Our eyes, like tiny prison windows
From which we gaze, yearning
A life sentence in our bodies

The sun, uncompromisingly hot
Roasting the tourist
In his ugly American uniform

A little green lizard-thing
A Godzilla wanna-be
Scampered into the bush, startled

My accomplishments
My achievements
In spite of you

The Italian honey-bee
Busy, buzzing
Making Italian honey

The sawdust smells
Of healthy wood
But a murdered tree

Little lizard
Stiff with the cold night
Couldn't run from the boy

The eternal beauty of Tuscany
Makes me feel so
Temporary

The caffeine and alcohol
Battled fiercely in his bloodstream
He just sat and enjoyed the show

What a lovely afternoon
A strong Italian coffee
With a view to the sea

The American city
Offers me no pride nor beauty
Only inspiration for ugly poetry

If I could only gaze into those
Hazel eyes, I'd be forced to see
The reflection of the old and ugly

The howling of a Tuscan dog
Reminds me of the California hills,
Beautiful midnight coyote songs

It makes no difference
What I write, paint or sing for you
You will never find me or love me

Climbing along the Cecina jetty
The sea's music
Crashing on the rocks, into my ears

I must create to free my soul
If only a little
For no one really cares of poetry

If I could sing,
I'd sing you a song
That would even inspire the angels

Let me dive into those hazel eyes
Swim within your natural beauty
Bask in your perfection

Keep that mirror away
For I am a monster, old
Not worthy of your virgin heart

The little boy
Pasting fresh flowers on paper
Was angry when they dried away

Human nature
Is born of mother nature
But is so much more contemptable

If I spew ugly art
It is just a reaction
To your cultural vomit

Definition of an old fool:
The middle-aged man whose eyes
Still follow pretty young panties

Don't awake that longing
For it can't be controlled
And can only be expressed in pain

The little boy playing on the beach
Lost his shoe to the tide
And his tears became the sea

Heaven is easy to define:
Painting and writing
In a little Tuscan village

I walk a nameless, dusty road
I neither know nor care
For the time of day

The beauty of gravity
Manifested in the way
It pulls on her breasts

The little crabs scampered
Sideways
Avoiding the grip of the little boy

A seagull swooped
And rose, disappointed
With the floating coke can

A strong wind of salty tasting air
The smell of a seafood restaurant
Nearby, sand in my shoes

A wood of pines
Leaning away from the coast
As if they don't like salty sea air

The black stone of Cecina beach
Was warm on the tourist's
Buttocks

If I piss into the Ganges
Will I become one
With Beatle George?

Endless rolling hills, grapes
Stone landscape and olive trees
Birthplace of a true human culture

Oh, to be a little boy again
And be fascinated for hours
By the most mundane things

A bubble floating through the air
Colors translucent, beauty
Radiant eyes of a happy little boy

Don't awake that longing
For it can't be controlled
And can only be expressed in pain

How can you punish the Jew
For executing your savior
When Jesus never existed?

Lazy afternoon walk with my dog
She's gettin' old, I can tell
She doesn't see that cat

Sun-baked and warm Tuscan tiles
A welcome relief
For these north European feet

If you were created
In your god's image
Then religion can't be true

A little boy exploring his world
Collecting pretty rocks
That I have to carry home

The endless buzzing and chirping
Life's music
Too often falling upon deaf ears

A little hunger in the gut
Is healthy
For the artist's inspiration

Tired legs, sore feet
A lasting testimony
To my cultural apologies

TV, tractor pulls, fast food
A fat wench in polyester
A testimony to ugly culture

Early morning buzzing
A hungry bumble bee
A holiday style alarm clock

A lonely green turtle
Saw me and quickly dived
Murky water of a deserted fountain

The timelessness of the Italian air
As it arrogantly knows
It need prove nothing more

A bubble floating through the air
Express colors translucent, beauty
Until it pops on a branch

A moss-covered branch
Crunched under my foot
And annoyed several ants

A sunny Siena day
Dodging faceless tourists
Dodging myself?

Aggressive, the black scorpion
Wildly stabbed its ugly thorn
At the side of the glass container

The eternal beauty of Tuscany
Serves as a sober reminder
We are all no more than guests

The little boy learned with joy
To skip flat rocks on into the sea
One, two, three, I beat you!

Rows of olive trees
Preparing olives, preparing oil
For my future dinners

Gigantic grasshopper
Buzzing by my ear
Thought it was a helicopter

True holiday luxury
Not knowing, nor caring
For the time of day

Beautifully formed, yet nameless
Stone, I'll name you
Butch, the stone

The freckles started popping
With the first spring sun
As ornery as the boy himself

Blue eyes bubbled with questions
Of life: why, where, what, how?
Daddy, buy me a glass of soda

Just by judging the cooking
Italian marriages
Must be the world's most stable

A long jetty of huge stones
A playground for boys
And little crabs

Round stone covered in green
Seaweed, looks a bit like
A Mediterranean Beatles wig

The little boy collecting
Pretty stones on the beach
Each more valuable than the last

The long jetty of huge stones
Where little boys and little crabs
Play games of hide and seek

The Italian sunshine
Brings out the play in the boy
And lets his red hair glow

Endless rows of Italian grape vines
To make red wine
For German tourists

A little red-headed boy
So new to this world
Discovering its beauty, new

Florence

The perfection of Van Gogh
Was crowned by his act
Of self-destruction

I'd rather die
Than forget those few minutes
As I loved you in my daydreams

That naked dead poet
Glaring with contempt at me
Through middle aged, mirror eyes

Italian farms
With Italian chickens
Do they cluck in Italian?

I am as a dog
Domesticated and dumb
Worthy of a kick in the ribs

Useless! Useless!
An old artist
Falling in love again

I still wouldn't want to be
A beat poet, 'cause means
That I'd probably be dead by now

The rotting, dying artist
Too dumb to fight the tide
Too ugly to win true love

Don't insult your natural beauty
And down to earth perfection
With cosmetics of want

If only I could strip myself
To pure nakedness
And howl with the best

Evolution:
From angry young punk
To angry old poet

Useless! Useless!
The artist
Standing in line at Burger King

Coke advertisements prove
America won the battle
But lost the war

Smoldering, discarded cigar
Mingled its sweet smoke
With the exhaust of the traffic

I'd rather die than
Let the world soften the imprint
Of those hazel eyes on my soul

That exquisite temptation
Only magnified the panic
Of missing the boat

A subtle glance, large hazel eyes
Beauty beyond comprehension
Twenty years and worlds apart

America, yes, I've deserted you
For I prefer real hippos
And beer that doesn't taste of piss

Strange swamp amphibian
Swimming through murky water
Wonders why he has legs

Better than a lottery win
The privilege, gazing into those
Eyes, in love for a lifetime

This domesticated life
Is light years from where
My dreams tried to lead me

The curse of the romantic artist
The daily routine of life
Disappoints his dreams

His old eyes grew weary
With yearning and searching
For one more glimpse of hazel

Sterzing

The more the alcohol
The better the poetry, but
The worse the poet's handwriting

Traffic jams and a long drive home
Liquor store already closed, damn!
My holiday is over!

If there is a heaven
Then they serve Italian ice-cream
Every day, non-stop

A mini volume
Inspiration on the way
Poetry to go

Useless! Useless!
A heavy smoker
In the crisp Alpine air

In a perfect world
Poetry books
Would be on best seller lists

Alpine pines
Clinging to mountain sides
Basking in the fresh mountain air

My Italian blood surges
Longing for a home
Like a yearly holiday magnet

His eyes grew weary with travel
And his mind snapped back into
The mode of tired routine

A weakling could
Tried and tried
But got caught between two alps

Butt pocket poetry
Inspiration in a gas station
When no one is looking

The Alpine lizard,
If he exists,
Spends most of his time sleeping

Punk rock: perfect music
Plop art: perfect punk art
Western haiku: perfect punk poetry

„Once upon a time"?
How about „Once below a time"
Or even „Once next to a time"

The buzzing sound, coming closer
He ducked his head just in time
A giant grasshopper near miss

A long drive, a cold beer
The beginning
Of a perfect holiday

Pure happiness:
Watching your little boy
Explore his world

A law of nature:
The more the alcohol
The better the poetry

The lucky poet writes to strangers
Most though only write to lovers,
And friends

Once upon a time
A poet began writing
And never stopped

Basel

If only I could see
In all their eyes
If they would have said „yes"

The huge train station hall
Echoed with the pleas
Of the hungry beggar

A hustle bustle
Foreign city
A tourist walking in circles

A field full of yellow flowers
Ignored by everyone but me
And some farmer somewhere

Unknown hazel eyed beauty
Somewhere....
What are you doing right now?

A beggar's banquet
The dried-up crust
Of a day-old, rancid Big Mac ™

The modern art was huge
Covering an entire wall
No one looked

A large cold beer
Is the tourist's reward
For his aimless wanderings

Hamburg

A colourful pheasant
Strutted into the road, so
Close to death, too dumb to know

His ideas, thoughts, scrambled
Like so much scrambled eggs
At a sleazy midwestern diner

The sunshine hatches freckles
The red hair positively glows!
My boy, my joy

Creating
Did help him feel better
If only for awhile

Those eternal red bricks
And such quaint thatched roofs
Northern German charm

You might be cocky, and wild
And yes, you do look sharp
But you're still a chicken

High altitude sunshine
A chirpy little boy at my side
Why can't I feel happy?

A holiday nearing its death
A time for sorrow and goodbyes
A time for travel stress

Calculating crash statistics
The nervous flyer
Clung to his seat in fear

Reeperbahn rodeo
Ride the spread eagle
And pay through your teeth

Such limitless energy
A love of life
Was I ever a little boy?

Up here you can't touch me
You fat-assed arrogant
Son of a stupid bitch

The sun was so bright
Reflecting off the plane's wings
Into the little boys excited eyes

The clouds, like cotton candy
Inspiration for so many
Clumsy analogies

The jets rumbled, shook
He felt nervous
And drank of his beer

The waves splashed
The boats rocked
The stomachs turned

Reality of distances
And a sad goodbye
End of a family holiday

Waiting, waiting, waiting
Yet more waiting
Now you may board

His ideas, thoughts scrambled
Blotting what he could to paper
In no particular order

You could tell, he had no ticket
Nervous glances at the doors
And ready to flee

Those pretty blue eyes
That endlessly curious little brain
At work, my boy, my joy

A green tourist
Tries to keep his lunch down
While smiling for the camera

I collect stressful problems
When one is solved
I have the next already lined up

That subway tunnel smelled
Of standing water and piss
And drying graffiti paint

A big city harbour, characterized
By the sailors, with a wad of cash
And a block on their shoulders

I only ask for peace of mind
From all of life's problems
From myself

That subway tunnel smelled
Of long ago parties and excitement
Of untamed youth and pure dreams

Such a beautiful day
Up here, above the clouds
Above that rainstorm

Old man reading
Didn't bother to notice
As air turbulence rattled his paper

Only in his dreams did he dare
Smash that arrogant nose
Of the Mercedes driver

I ask not of money
Nor wealth, nor health
Just peace of mind

Swinemünde

Some of the world's greatest
Literature is lost, forever
Because a pencil wasn't at hand

Rows and rows of crops
To be eaten, then shat
Life can be so meaningless

No bills, no stress, nor bitchy wife
No asshole boss either, only sleep
Maybe death isn't so bad after all

That's so disgusting
I wouldn't even wanna
Piss on it

Beautiful woman on the bus,
Are you the love of my life?
Please tell me, I need to know

Graffiti:
The poor man's
Advertisement

Look like an aged punk-rocker
And you have less chance
Of getting mugged

The problem with bagpipe bands
You never really know
If they're good or not

Is it just the alcohol,
Or all the Polish women
Really all so pretty?

That Polish citizen
Belches
A universal language

Such a pretty town
Abandoned
By its citizens

Cross a street
Cross a river
Cross a border

Let me walk those dark,
Once forbidden streets
Where communists once ruled

I thought the train was coming
But it was only the chirp
Of a Polish cricket

The former promised land
Now only promises
Cheap cigarettes, diseased whores

Another few steps
Another country
To add to my list

Both feet planted
On each side of a border
I am now truly international

Assholes speak
In a universal language
Unfortunately I'm a native speaker

Bauhaus on sale
Buy one, get one free
For every communist

Time for more Polish alcohol
A Polish meal, a Polish bed
Goodnight, Poland

Put your pen away
You've fulfilled your duty
For today

Harz

There are more trees than people
They should rebel
And overthrow mankind

She came in through
The bathroom window
Maybe she had to piss?

On a hot summer day
He dreamed of tasting salty sweat
That collected between her breasts

Just let me mope, just let me stare
Just let me...
Just let my cry

Everything is relative
Including,
My disappointment in you

Imagine a world
Governed by trees
Imagine a perfect world

Like water to an ugly color paint
Put distance between us
Water down that indifference

Silence echoed through the house
Testament to the absence
Of a little boy

Why shouldn't I write this?
You don't care
And will never read it anyway

For once,
A good day
I take what I can get

Don't speak of me
In the simple past
I am not (yet) a corpse

For your birthday
I thought of you
You still exist in my heart

If the city is a jungle
And I am Tarzan
Does that make you Jane?

A little girl grew up once
Became such a pretty lady
And made her daddy proud

A real „love story"
Is one of endurance
Compromise and limitless patience

No, I'm not from Mars
Just an old man
In a punk-rock T-shirt

Beaded sweat
Collected, then ran
Salted drips on his lips

Youth is present perfect
Death is the simple past
Old age has arrived

A day spent exploring a city
Too tired to move
Too tired to think

More and more
I see you in me
And that gives me the creeps

Take the ball and run
When you can
I am on a writing roll!

Vienna

Our band is a scape-goat
For your unfulfilled dreams
And bad B.O.

The throbbing behind his eye
Obliterated all traces
Of interest or inspiration

Raindrops rolling upward
Pushed by the wind
Against the windshield

A beat your meat manifesto
Tubthumping all the way
To the bank, in a stupid mode

Our gear
Won't create stars
But at least headaches

Early sober Saturday morning
Wandering the streets of Vienna
Looking for coffee

They drank to their stars
Danced and had fun
Contributing to the revelation

If you really loved me
You'd show me
And give me a call

The background noise of a band
And a refrigerator humming
And I could finally sleep

Europe is my home
My blood and my intellect
And my future

I'm such a liberal artist
I won't even censor myself
As I'm sure you can tell

Are these scribbles good poetry?
Just be happy you don't have to
Try to decipher the handwriting